AMERICANA

CONTENTS

T0081548

— PIANO LEVEL —
LATE INTERMEDIATE/EARLY ADVANCED

ISBN 978-1-4234-1790-3

HAL•LEONARD®
CORPORATION
7777 W. BLUEMOUND RD. P.O.BOX 13819 MILWAUKEE, WI 53213

In Australia Contact:
Hal Leonard Australia Pty. Ltd.
22 Taunton Drive   P.O. Box 5130
Cheltenham East, 3192 Victoria, Australia
Email: ausadmin@halleonard.com

Visit Hal Leonard Online at
www.halleonard.com

Visit Phillip at
www.phillipkeveren.com

ARKANSAS TRAVELER

Southern American Folksong
Arranged by Phillip Keveren

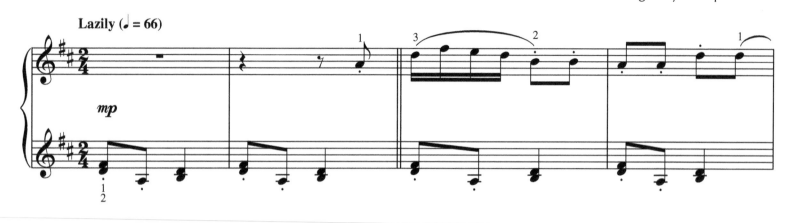

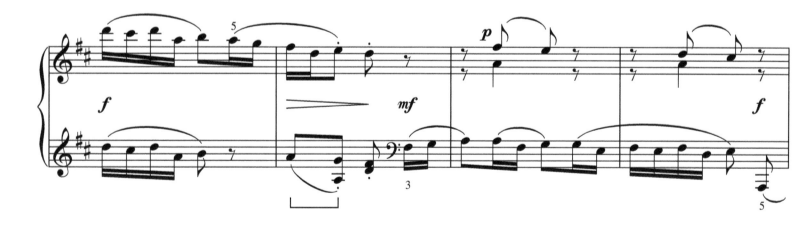

Tempo I

BEAUTIFUL DREAMER

Words and Music by STEPHEN C. FOSTER
Arranged by Phillip Keveren

BLACK IS THE COLOR OF MY TRUE LOVE'S HAIR

Southern Appalachian Folksong
Arranged by Phillip Keveren

With yearning (♩ = 84-92)

DEEP RIVER

African-American Spiritual
Based on Joshua 3
Arranged by Phillip Keveren

DOWN IN THE VALLEY

Traditional American Folksong
Arranged by Phillip Keveren

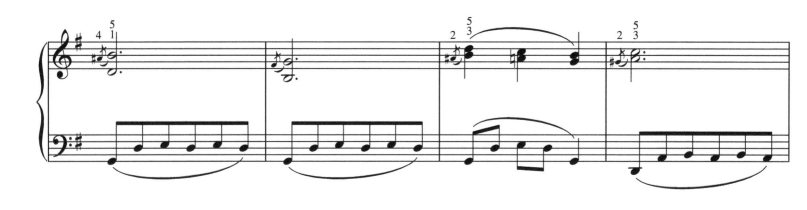

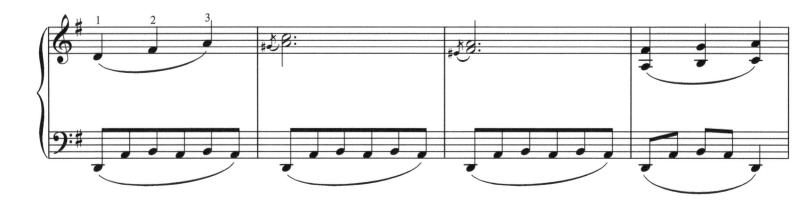

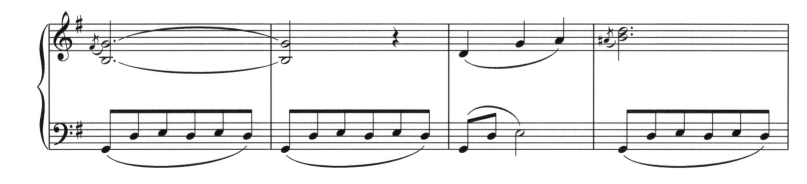

Briskly (♩. = 104)

HUSH, LITTLE BABY

Carolina Folk Lullaby
Arranged by Phillip Keveren

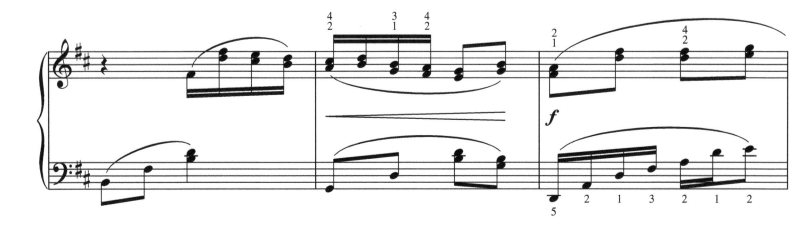

JEANIE WITH THE LIGHT BROWN HAIR

Words and Music by STEPHEN C. FOSTER
Arranged by Phillip Keveren

OH! SUSANNA

Words and Music by STEPHEN C. FOSTER
Arranged by Phillip Keveren

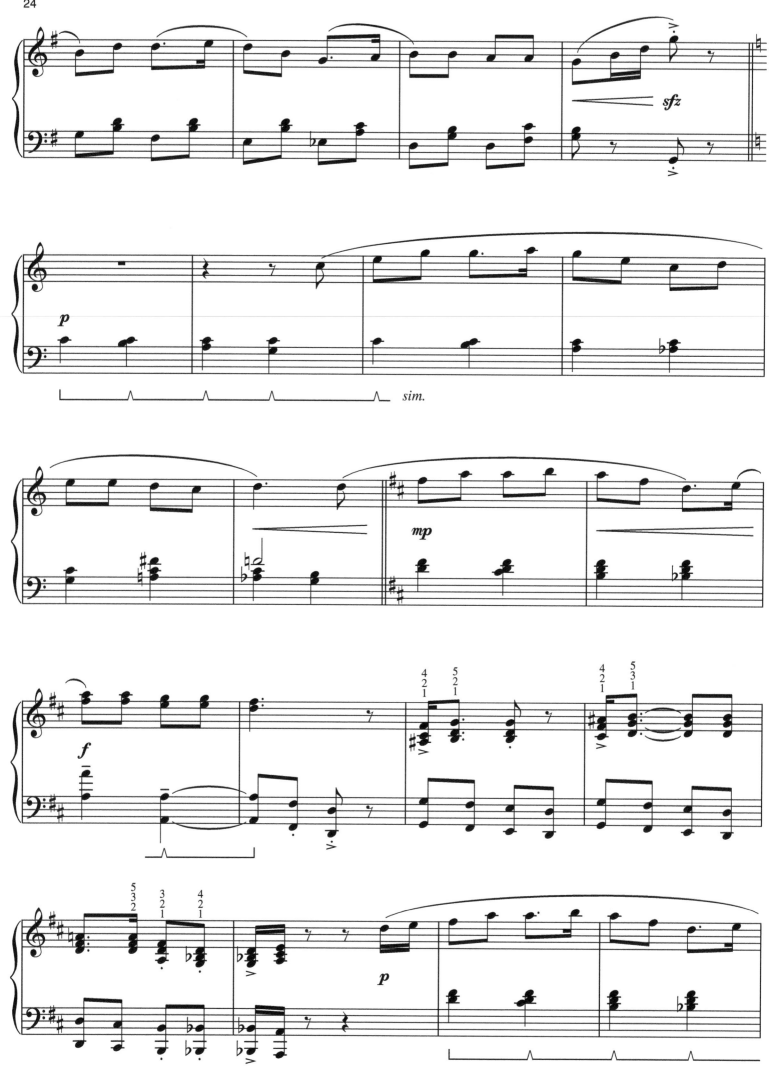

THE RED RIVER VALLEY

Traditional American Cowboy Song
Arranged by Phillip Keveren

SHENANDOAH

American Folksong
Arranged by Phillip Keveren

Slowly, with great freedom (♩ = 63-69)

With pedal

With motion

SHE'LL BE COMIN' 'ROUND THE MOUNTAIN

Traditional
Arranged by Phillip Keveren

Brightly (♩ = 116)

SIMPLE GIFTS

Traditional Shaker Hymn
Arranged by Phillip Keveren

Simply (♩ = 104-112)

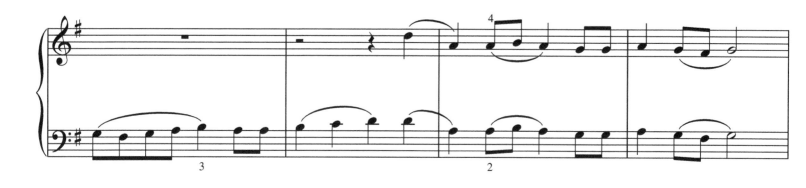

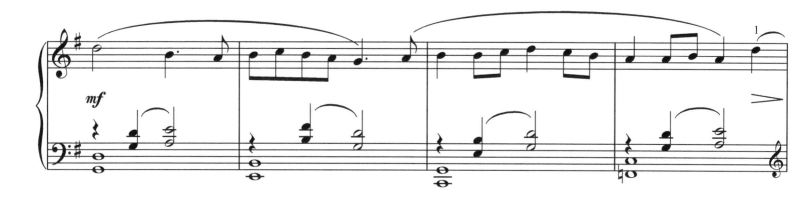

Driving (♩ = 200)

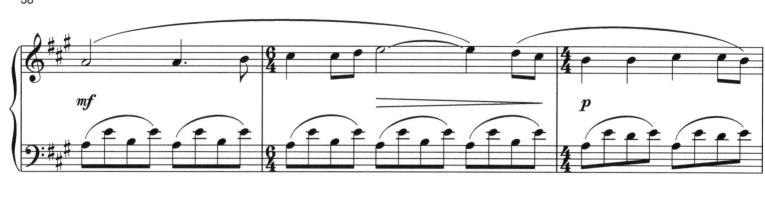

Briskly, in 1 (♩. = 63)

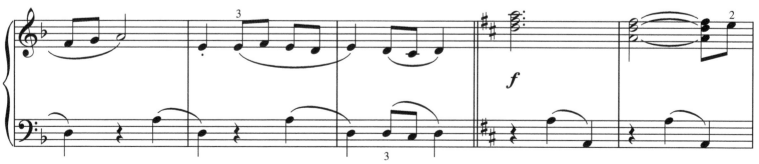

WHEN THE SAINTS GO MARCHING IN

Words by KATHERINE E. PURVIS
Music by JAMES M. BLACK
Arranged by Phillip Keveren

Jazz Waltz (♩ = 168)

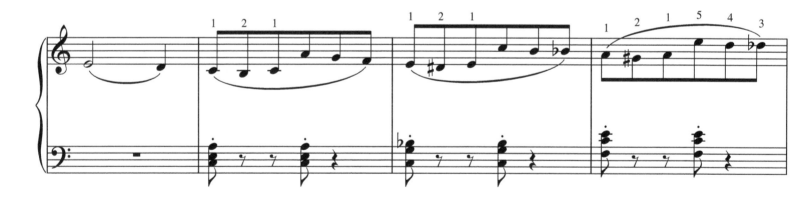

WONDROUS LOVE

Southern American Folk Hymn
Arranged by Phillip Keveren

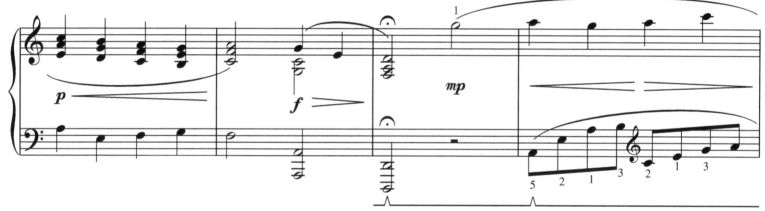

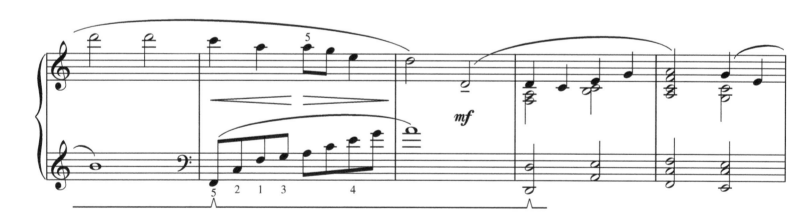

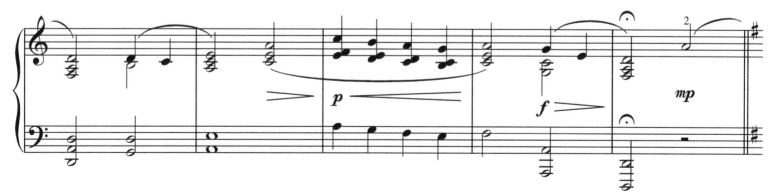

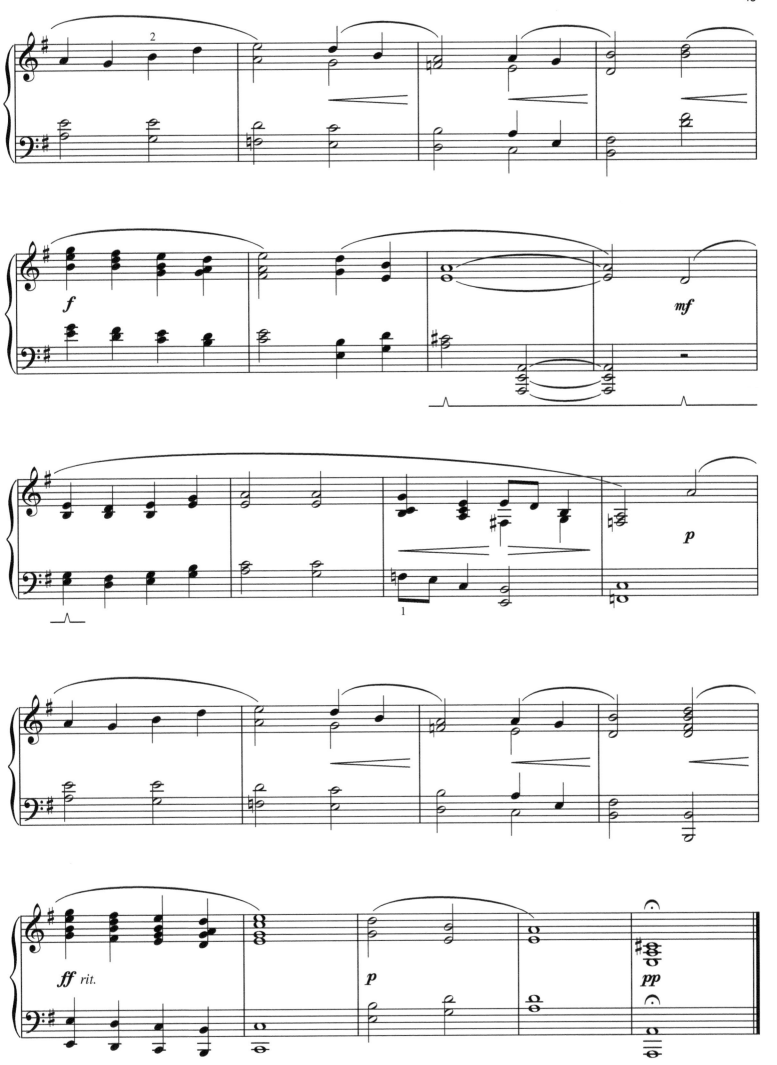

WAYFARING STRANGER

Southern American Folk Hymn
Arranged by Phillip Keveren

Più mosso

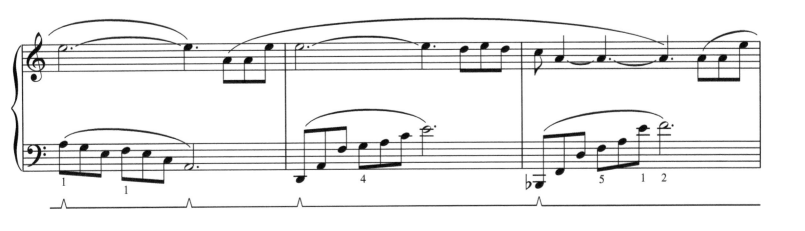